T0078143

# FAMILIARITY

# ?

With God, With Man, With the Adversary; All Will Surprise You.
**GOD DOES MORE WHEN WE ARE FLEXIBLE**

PAULINE ADONGO

WESTBOW
PRESS®
A DIVISION OF THOMAS NELSON
& ZONDERVAN

Scripture taken from the King James Version of the Bible.

Scripture taken from the New King James Version®. Copyright © 1982 by Thomas Nelson. Used by permission. All rights reserved.

Scripture quotations marked (NIV) are taken from the Holy Bible, New International Version®, NIV®. Copyright © 1973, 1978, 1984, 2011 by Biblica, Inc.™ Used by permission of Zondervan. All rights reserved worldwide. www.zondervan. com The "NIV" and "New International Version" are trademarks registered in the United States Patent and Trademark Office by Biblica, Inc.™

Scripture quotations taken from the New American Standard Bible® (NASB), Copyright © 1960, 1962, 1963, 1968, 1971, 1972, 1973, 1975, 1977, 1995 by The Lockman Foundation. Used by permission. www.Lockman.org

Scripture quotations are taken from the Holy Bible, New Living Translation, copyright ©1996, 2004, 2007, 2013, 2015 by Tyndale House Foundation. Used by permission of Tyndale House Publishers, Inc., Carol Stream, Illinois 60188. All rights reserved.

WestBow Press books may be ordered through booksellers or by contacting:

WestBow Press
A Division of Thomas Nelson & Zondervan
1663 Liberty Drive
Bloomington, IN 47403
www.westbowpress.com
1 (866) 928-1240

ISBN: 978-1-5127-8336-0 (sc)
ISBN: 978-1-5127-8337-7 (e)

Library of Congress Control Number: 2017905819

Print information available on the last page.

WestBow Press rev. date: 04/21/2017

I am dedicating this book to my brothers
Joseph Oriko and Eliud Omollo.
Individually, you have both inspired me. I love you dearly, Polly.

Also, dedicating this book to a special long-
term friend; Philip Anyango.
Thanks for nourishing authentic friendship of over 20 years.

# ENDORSEMENT

"***Familiarity***" *is a commonplace in the church today. Your book is very helpful in understanding how detrimental it can be to spiritual growth, individually, and even corporately. I am blessed beyond words by every chapter and content of this book. It is a must read for any Christian worker or leader who really value growth, continuity, and relevance in the kingdom of God.*

*I particularly appreciate how you challenge a deep consider our hearts and motives to recognize the pride and self-righteousness there. Using personal stories and enlightening examples from the Bible, you demonstrate how familiarity breeds pride; which interferes with a close relationship with God and reveals how to overcome pride and become more like Jesus. The book is insightful, educative and very informative about familiarity.*

*Again thanks,*
*Denis Odhiambo Okang, MA, LPCC*
*Senior Pastor, LifeSpring International Church, Lehigh Valley, Pennsylvania*

# TABLE OF CONTENTS

SECTION III
CONCLUSION

# SECTION I

# CAUSES OF FAMILIARITY

≈

# CHAPTER 1

# INTRODUCTION

≈

While reflecting on my personal life one winter evening, I received a revelation about the topic of this book. Familiarity is a great hindrance to life! Familiarity stunts our spiritual and natural growth.

Habitually, I listen to the Bible app, Christian teachings, or music while working out in the gym. On this evening, the Scripture I was reflecting on was Deuteronomy 1: 34-46, which says:

> *And the Lord heard the sound of your words, and was angry, and took an oath, saying, 'Surely not one of these men of this evil generation shall see that good land of which I swore to give to your fathers, except Caleb the son of Jephunneh; he shall see it, and to him and his children I am giving the land on which he walked, because he wholly followed the Lord.' The Lord was also angry with me for your sakes, saying, 'Even you shall not go in there. Joshua the son of Nun, who stands before you, he shall go in there. Encourage him, for he shall cause Israel to inherit it.*
>
> *Moreover, your little ones and your children, who you say will be victims, who today have no knowledge of good and evil, they shall go in there; to them I will give it, and*

*they shall possess it. But as for you, turn and take your journey into the wilderness by the Way of the Red Sea.'*

*Then you answered and said to me, 'We have sinned against the Lord; we will go up and fight, just as the Lord our God commanded us.' And when every one of you had girded on his weapons of war, you were ready to go up into the mountain.*

*And the Lord said to me, 'Tell them, "Do not go up nor fight, for I am not among you; lest you be defeated before your enemies." So, I spoke to you; yet you would not listen, but rebelled against the command of the Lord, and presumptuously went up into the mountain. And the Amorites who dwelt in that mountain came out against you and chased you as bees do, and drove you back from Seir to Hormah. Then you returned and wept before the Lord, but the Lord would not listen to your voice nor give ear to you.*

*So, you remained in Kadesh many days, according to the days that you spent there (NJKV).*

Initially, I was trying to figure out why the Israelites would repeatedly disobey God after experiencing His deliverance and seeing His power repeatedly. In fact, it got to a point that I too became frustrated with the Israelites. These people saw God part the seas for them to walk through. They saw the Egyptian armies thwarted before their eyes. They experienced God's divine protection and preservation, and they had continuous supply of food, clothing and security. They were accompanied by God's glory and pillar of cloud that went before and after them. The Israelites lacked no good thing. They heard the voice of the Lord and witnessed the consequences of disobeying God. Whenever God chastened them, they were quick to repent and send Moses to speak to God on their behalf. Based on their experience with

God, the Israelites knew to inquire from the Lord especially on the matters of war.

As I listened to further, I noticed similar attitudes and behaviors of the Israelites in the book of Judges when Joshua sent them to spy in the city of Ai. The spies returned with such a relaxed attitude, recommending that only few soldiers be sent to attack Ai, but what a disappointment they got.

> *Now Joshua sent men from Jericho to Ai, which is near Beth Aven to the east of Bethel, and told them, "Go up and spy out the region." So, the men went up and spied out Ai. When they returned to Joshua, they said, "Not all the army will have to go up against Ai. Send two or three thousand men to take it and do not weary the whole army, for only a few people live there." ⁴ So about three thousand went up; but they were routed by the men of Ai, who killed about thirty-six of them. They chased the Israelites from the city gate as far as the stone quarries and struck them down on the slopes. At this the hearts of the people melted in fear and became like water. Then Joshua tore his clothes and fell facedown to the ground before the ark of the LORD, remaining there till evening. The elders of Israel did the same, and sprinkled dust on their heads. (Joshua. 7:2-6, NIV).*

I took interest in the event at Ai, slowing down the treadmill to tune into the story. As I adjusted my pace, I heard the Holy Spirit say "familiarity; the Israelites were familiar with the ways of God." I smiled, thanked the Holy Spirit, and zoned out to now reflect on my own life.

This event happened in February 2016. Early in the year I had zoned out to reflect on other personal goals and how I would juggle or structure and balance the time spent in each area effectively to accomplish all goals. As I slowed down on the treadmill, I heard "flexibility with

God produces much!" I thanked the Holy Spirit again. You see, I am naturally very structured. I run on a tight schedule and things must align that way. Therefore, when the Spirit said, "Flexibility with God produces much," I could relate this to my own life and tie flexibility as solution to familiarity. I recorded this experience in my journal on February 6th, 2016.

Initially, I thought the topic would be suitable for my weekly social media blog. So, I decide to write the blog for posting, but as I wrote the Holy Spirit continued to reveal more. Interestingly, the revelation was on the spiritual Christian life as well as daily life application. As you read on, there are key areas to consider and questions to reflect upon in each chapter. It is my hope that from them you will evaluate areas of complacency in your walk with God or desire for more as you rely totally on God.

# CHAPTER 2

# THE UNTEACHABLE SPIRIT

≈

One of the causes of familiarity is the unteachable spirit or attitude. This normally presents with an "I know" attitude where the believer is convinced he or she has all he or she may need and thus does require additional information, ideas, and suggestions. Parents may argue that this attitude is limited to teenagers or young adults, but the story of the Israelites in Deuteronomy and Judges prove otherwise. The unteachable spirit can be found in mature Christians, including those in leadership or ministerial offices.

Pride and arrogance commonly accompany an unteachable person. You will realize that such people are comfortable with where they are and are resistant to change. Familiarity in such instances commonly manifests in phrases such as: "We have done it before," This is how we do it around here," "I can do that better," or "Who are you tell me what to do?" The "I can do it better" attitude is normally in partnership with the defiance pride of satan himself. Such people will also despise advice from others, especially is they think they are more qualified.

When pride and familiarity are combined, it breeds a false, overly self-confident attitude that makes one think they know it all. Those with a familiarity spirit may present as extremely smart beyond counselling. They may even be justifying their attitude with statements such as "I have more experience; I have doing this for a long time." I must say that both in ministry and in the work environment, people with the unteachable spirit are the most challenging people to work with.

Familiarity presents in someone with an unteachable spirit as being comfortable and familiar with what they know or have. A rebellious person can also be unteachable to because rebellious people tend object counsel do whatever they want. This creates no room for new information or ideas to advance; resulting in no spiritual or natural growth!

## *Consider This*

God desires still desires to show more and do more with us through the Holy Spirit. He calls this fruitfulness. "*Call to Me, and I will answer you, and show you great and mighty things, which you do not know*" *(Jer. 33:3, NJKV)*. To do this, we must empty ourselves of what we know or have and receive more from Him. This is the removal of the old wine skin for the new wine to be poured in us. Old wine skins and wines are the old information, ideas, processes, and systems that we may have. This is not to say that old is bad, however, progress may require fine-tuning, revising, updating, or even getting rid of the old. Jesus Christ explained this teaching in Luke 5:36-39:

> *Then He spoke a parable to them: "No one puts a piece from a new garment on an old one; otherwise the new makes a tear, and the piece that was taken out of the new does not match the old. And no one puts new wine into old wineskins; or else the new wine will burst the wineskins and be spilled, and the wineskins will be ruined. But new wine must be put into new wineskins, and both are preserved. And no one, having drunk old wine, immediately desires new; for he says, 'The old is better'" (NJKV).*

God has given us free will and the choice to attain more for great fruitiness is on us not on God. When we are open to receive from God, He pours more. He promises to fill those who hunger for righteousness.

*Reflection:* Do you have a teachable spirit or attitude?

# CHAPTER 3

# ASSUMPTIOUS STEREOTYPICAL ATTITUDES

≈

Have you ever been in the company of people who treated you differently? By being treated differently, I mean being ignored, being unacknowledged, watching others receive preferential treatment, etc.? However, once you present yourself or do something elaborate that the same people did not expect, their attitude towards you changes. Such attitudes, behaviors and reactions are based on assumptions!

You can be very familiar with something or someone and conclude or expect specific outcomes based on assumptions, only to be quite surprised. This is the surprise the Israelites encountered in Ai in Joshua 7. The spies assumed Ai's army was too small. They stereotyped it, thinking: "Every small army is weak and does not need a large force to attack." Joshua sent spies to scout Ai, and the spies returned with the report: "Oh Joshua, do not bother sending in a big army, just sent small battalion, the city is small, a smaller army should handle it." Well, the smaller Israeli army went to Ai, but Ai's army killed thirty-six Israeli soldiers and chased them far off! The spies underestimated Ai's strength. This was a stereotype. The spies believed smaller cities have no power and only need little or no ammunition. The outcome was defeat, shame, and fear.

We can miss the "big picture" that God wants to do with us when we assume things or develop stereotypical attitudes. The Bible is full of near misses and missed opportunities on the move of God and what God wanted to do. The Pharisees and Sadducees, the religious sect, missed Jesus because they saw Him dining with Jesus. They assumed the coming Messiah would dine with them. You would think that after the three wise men followed the stars to confirm Jesus was born in Bethlehem, they still missed Jesus because they kept arguing that Jesus was from Galilee. To date they are still waiting for the Messiah to come from Bethlehem.

Naaman the king may have missed his healing if he would have insisted that he needed to dip himself in cleaner waters rather than the muddy Jordan River. In fact, it took the servant girl to convince him 2 Kings 5:13. You may miss out on a blessing or a move of God because you only believe that only prophets, pastors, and apostles should pray for you. You may miss up during worship because you only believe worship group or leader to usher you to God's presence. You may miss out of God when you skip church because your favorite pastor is not preaching that day.

We can really miss God if we assume that He will move in a certain way or do things in a certain way. I caution on this now more than ever because God is moving differently, radically, and even more quickly in this millennial age than ever before. The advance in technology is allowing for dissemination of the gospel and evangelistic efforts much more quickly.

To move with God, and to grow and advance spiritually and naturally, we should accept that God may not use what He used before and be open to the diverse forums God will communicate and work with us. If we hold unto things needing to be done just a certain way or the idea that the Holy Spirit must just work in a certain way, we will miss out on God. More concerning, by doing this, we will be restricting or limiting the much needed full flow of the Holy Spirit. We also have the potential of reverting to the "works of the flesh" when we focus our outcomes to assumptions and stereotypical attitudes.

## *Consider This*

God is a respecter of no person; Job 34:19. To God everybody is equal, and He chooses whom to use. *"Then Peter opened his mouth and said: 'In truth I perceive that God shows no partiality. In every nation, whoever fears Him and works righteousness is accepted by Him'" (Acts 10:34-35, NJKV).*

God can move through anything and anybody, title or no title, big or small; these are irrelevant to God because He created us all. Romans 2:10 is a great encouragement whenever I reflect on equality in God. It says: "But glory, honor, and peace to everyone who works what is good, to the Jew first and to the Greek" (NKJV). There is no partiality with God. Therefore, be open to any person, value, and door God will open. Do not underestimate any vessel God will use to bless you.

*Reflection:* What assumptions have you gathered throughout your Christianity?

Have you developed any stereotypical attitudes that have caused you to miss out to God? Are you ready to renounce assumptions and stereotyping?

# CHAPTER 4

# PAST EXPERIENCES

≈

We can develop familiarity in our Christian walk, in relationship, and overall in life from assumptions that what worked in the past will work again. When we develop a mindset that we have come to full understanding of the ways of God and conclude that He will move the same way He moved before, we can miss out on God. Looking back, whether on good things or bad things, can cripple the present and disable the future should you stay solely focused on them.

From personal experience, I've come to learn that God may want the same desired outcome as before, but He may not use the same methods to get you there. I recall desiring to seek God in prayer over a period of adversity in my life. I thought I could do the same things I did over six years ago, but I was wrong. The Holy Spirit led me a totally different way this time around. Now I know that He did this because He wanted to expose things in my life as well as teach me new things, and the only way I needed to experience these were through new processes.

Jesus demonstrated perfectly the application of different ministries to heal and deliver others. For one blind man, he spat on his eyes and commanded them to see, to the other he touched the eyes and the blind saw. To Lazarus, Jesus called him out of the tomb. Yet to the young girl, Jesus went to her room and prayed for her, and she became alive again! God diversifies and uses new ways to minister to us and to others.

The problem of "past successes" is what Moses encountered that eventually cost him dearly. Moses was pressured by the Israelite in the dessert. You recall, the Israelites demanded water from Moses because they were thirsty. Previously, prior to this incident, they had cried out for water. Then, Moses sought God and the God asked Moses to strike a rock and water flowed from the rock.

After travelling some distance again, the Israelites got thirsty and demanded water from Moses. God told Moses to "speak to the rock, not strike as before." Instead of Moses following God's guidance, he stroked the rock in anger and water flowed. However, although His desired outcome was obtained, this is how God had desired for it to done.

> And the LORD spoke to Moses, saying, Take the rod; and you and your brother Aaron assemble the congregation and speak to the rock before their eyes, that it may yield its water. You shall thus bring forth water for them out of the rock and let the congregation and their beasts drink." So, Moses took the rod from before the LORD, just as He had commanded him; and Moses and Aaron gathered the assembly before the rock. And he said to them, "Listen now, you rebels; shall we bring forth water for you out of this rock? Then Moses lifted up his hand and struck the rock twice with his rod; and water came forth abundantly, and the congregation and their beasts drank. But the LORD said to Moses and Aaron, "Because you have not believed Me, to treat Me as holy in the sight of the sons of Israel, therefore you shall not bring this assembly into the land which I have given them. "Those were the waters of Meribah, because the sons of Israel

*contended with the LORD, and He proved Himself holy among them. (Num. 20:7-13, NASB).*

Past experiences are also the reason why the religious sect, Pharisees and seduces, missed Jesus. This sect was looking for certain qualifications of a prophet in Jesus. Jesus though deemed a prophet by some, did not match the qualifications of what the religious sect were used to seeing a prophet despite Jesus performing signs and wonders and teaching them profoundly. Instead they persecuted Jesus and missed out on the Messiah.

## *Consider This*

If there is an area I would strongly caution it is in this: Never assume that God will use the same means towards a solution twice. Do not anticipate and rely on how God moved in the past and only stick to that. God may move that way, and He may not. In fact, if you approach any challenge with such attitude, you have already underestimated God's authority is from the beginning. It is as though you are starting in defeat already. He may visit in such a new and powerful way like new before. Actually, more and more He is doing this. God is progressive, He moves from glory to glory, new things to better and greater things. Hallelujah!

I encourage you to pray and ask God for a newer move and new things every day. If ministering, ask God for a fresh encounter every day. I believe God does this to show us different aspects of His power and His glory. This is what makes His manna or revelation or presence, fresh, new and sweet every time.

This is the Scripture that comes to mind on breaking reliance with past experiences and receiving new things from God: *"'For My thoughts are not your thoughts, nor are your ways My ways, says the Lord. 'For as the heavens are higher than the earth, so are My ways higher than your ways, and My thoughts than your thoughts'" (Isa. 55:8-9, NJKV).*

***Reflection:*** Are you stuck on past experiences? Do you always reference your previous encounters and which you reverted to having more of them? Is your ministry hanging on a phase or revival period? Has God exposed the new things to you and you have in turn questioned or surprised the move of the Holy Spirit because you were unsure?

# CHAPTER 5

# REPEAT SUCCESS AND SELF-RELIANCE

≈

After experiencing a series of repeated successes or increased blessings or breakthrough, it is very common to expect desired outcomes on an ongoing basis. Because of these desired outcomes, we can stop seeking guidance from the Holy Spirit and stop being dependent on God. This familiarity with success leads to self-reliance and personal strength void of God. The results of these types of familiarities have biblically been disastrous.

This was the case of Samson in. He thought that all the reasons he had provided Delilah about his strength were ineffective, because whenever Delilah called the philistines, Samson got up and attacked them. However, one day this he forgot that he had disclosed the real reason behind his strength. So, when Delilah called the philistines, Samson got up thinking he still had strength, but this time they got him. The Lord had left Samson, and Samson was unaware that the Lord had left him.

*When Delilah saw that he had told her everything, she sent word to the rulers of the Philistines, "Come back once more; for he has told all his heart." So, the lords of the Philistines came up to her and brought the money in her hand. Then she lulled him to sleep on her knees, and called for a man and had him shave off the seven locks of his head. Then she began to torment him, and his strength left him. And she said, "The Philistines are upon you, Samson!" So he awoke from his sleep, and said, "I will go out as before, at other times, and shake myself free!" But he did not know that the Lord had departed from him.*

*Then the Philistines took him and put out his eyes, and brought him down to Gaza. They bound him with bronze fetters, and he became a grinder in the prison (Judg. 16:18-21, NKJV).*

Familiarity stems from self-reliance, which depends on personal strength or self-effort. It ignores fellowship with and dependence on the Holy Spirit and focuses more on works. This type of familiarity is fueled by "past successes," which I explained in previous chapters. It is a false assumption of power that assumes that talents and gifts can still produce without the Holy Spirit. At this point the believer or minister becomes too comfortable in their calling and puts in no effort to grow spiritually. It is not uncommon to discover that such believers or ministers have no prayer life to study or read the Bible or have been compromised in some areas of their lives despite evidence of their gifts. Self-efforts may result in compromising and opening the door to deceptive spirits if one does not repent and pursue God.

The same attitude of familiarity based on past success and rebellion is what led to Israelites defeat by the Amorites. From the beginning of their journey to Canaan, they were used to inquiring from the Lord before they launched into war, obtaining approval to proceed, then fighting and winning. Their defeat by the Amorites this time was from pure reliance on past success and utter rebellion. They inquired of the Lord, God said "no," but they went anyway expecting God to defend them and give them a victory!

> *And the* Lord *said to me, 'Say to them, "Do not go up nor fight, for I am not among you; otherwise you will be defeated before your enemies."' So, I spoke to you, but you would not listen. Instead you rebelled against the command of the* Lord, *and acted presumptuously and went up into the hill country. The Amorites who lived in that hill country came out against you and chased you as bees do, and crushed you from Seir to Hormah. Then you returned and wept before the* Lord; *but the* Lord *did not listen to your voice nor give ear to you (Deut. 1: 42-45, NASB).*

This type of attitude is frankly appalling! Clearly it defies God's introductions but expects success and the desired outcome. It is no different than saying "God understands, that is what grace for, let me just launch in!" Oh, how that is so wrong! This dangerous attitude can camouflage as being familiar with the works and things of God based on our tenure in ministry or the depth of the gift we have. This familiarity spirit may manifest as: "I have been in ministry for this long," "I know how God moves," or even "Once I am on stage the power of God will fall in this fashion or the Holy Spirit will be here in fifteen minutes." Ridiculous! A fellow minister once inquired very plainly, "How can we order the Holy Spirit and contain Him to a timeframe?" This applies when we operate in the gift without the Holy Spirit. I would be mindful of the spirits working under such circumstances as these are signs of the last days. Which are living in now.

## *Consider This*

Already as believers, it is very disastrous to life a life that is not filled by or led by the Holy Spirit. More damaging though to the Body of Christ, is when we proclaim that are ministering at the direction of the Holy Spirit while we know very well that we are not.

Failure to submit to God's continues refining and pruning will result in not only being fruitless and presumptuous reliance on past success for fruitfulness. We must continually stay attached to our Main Branch, Jesus Christ. He is the tender of the vineyard. The pruning, chastening and refining are all essential to keep us filled with new oil. This requires that we stay hooked and focused on Him. This also requires total submission and obedience to the Holy Spirit. Although Jesus is the same yesterday, today and forever, His ways of working with and in us may vary. He is the potter and we are the clay. We must be conformable.

Ponder on these scriptures:
Zechariah 4:6 (NJKV): "So, he answered and said to me: This is the word of the Lord to Zerubbabel: Not by might nor by power, but by My Spirit, 'Says the Lord of hosts."

John 15:1-4 (NJKV): "I am the true vine, and My Father is the vinedresser. Every branch in Me that does not bear fruit He takes away; and every branch that bears fruit He prunes, that it may bear more fruit. You are already clean because of the word which I have spoken to you. Abide in Me, and I in you. As the branch, cannot bear fruit of itself, unless it abides in the vine, neither can you, unless you abide in Me."

John 15:5-8 (NJKV): "I am the vine, you are the branches. He who abides in Me, and I in him, bears much fruit; for without Me you can do nothing. If anyone does not abide in Me, he is cast out as a branch and is withered; and they gather them and throw them into the fire, and they are burned. If you abide in me, and My words abide in you, you will ask what you desire, and it shall be done for you. By this My Father is glorified, that you bear much fruit; so, you will be My disciples."

*Reflection:* Do you find yourself focusing on "works" of the flesh to produce spiritual results or get God's attention. Do you keep rehearsing past spiritual and personal successes? Are you struggling with obeying the Holy Spirit and/or counsel given by other believers or your pastor? How often do you read the Bible and pray? Are you Spirit filled and Spirit led.

# CHAPTER 6

# CONTENDING FOR EQUAL GIFTING WITHOUT PAYING THE PRICE

≈

Given the topic we are discussing in this chapter, I think it is best to start by providing clarification about being selected to become a follower of Jesus, being called and appointed into a ministerial office, and the distribution of spiritual gifts.

On being selected to be a follower of Jesus, the Bible says that even before being created we were already preordained and set apart by God. Through the salvation, we are each reconciled to God at the appointment of Jesus as our Shepherd. He foreknew us, therefore predestined us to be His children.

Romans 8:29-30 states: *"For whom He foreknew, He also predestined to be conformed to the image of His Son, that He might be the firstborn among many brethren. Moreover, whom He predestined, these He also called; whom He called, these He also justified; and whom He justified, and these He also glorified* (NJKV).

On the appointment of the ministerial offices, Jesus Christ does the appointment because He is the Head of the Church. (See Col. 1:18 and Eph. 5:23.) As the Head, He is the One who selects the apostles, prophets, pastors, evangelists, and teachers.

Ephesians 4:11-13 states: *"And He Himself gave some to be apostles, some prophets, some evangelists, and some pastors and teachers, for the equipping of the saints for the work of ministry, for the edifying of the body of Christ, till we all come to the unity of the faith and of the knowledge of the Son of God, to a perfect man, to the measure of the stature of the fullness of Christ"* (NKJV).

The Holy Spirit in turn distributes the gifts to support these offices; Wisdom, Knowledge, Faith, Healing, Miracles, Prophesy, Tongues and Interpretation of tongues. These can be found in 1 Corinthians 12:1-32.

The sole purpose for the offices and gifts of the Spirit are for the equipping and building of each believer to come to maturity and the fullness of Christ. The offices and the gifts are body parts connected to ONE HEAD, Jesus Christ. Each gift therefore works at the direction of that head and to the glory of the head.

Unity then becomes imperative for the body to be built. Designations of important gifts breeds division, halting the building of the church, which satan wants. "Importance" is the undertone of satan. He was kicked out of heaven because of it. Beware of importance. Importance says: "I do not need the head (Christ), and I do need the rest (others with gifts of the Spirit)." Gift seekers are prone to idolatry in their quest to want gifts that may not be necessarily assigned to them Scripture warns to seek the giver not the gift. (See 1 Cor. 16:22 and Matt. 6:22.)

All gifts are equally effective for the building up of each believer and the entire church. The reason why all gifts are connected and collectively working for the betterment of one body is because Christ is coming back for ONE BRIDE, ONE CHURCH. Though multifaceted and diverse, but the King is returning for one Church!

"The greatest gift of all is love" (1 Cor. 13:13b, NKJV). God is Love, Christ is Love. Spiritual gifts and offices must be administered from love, compassion, and mercy. If done without love, we are just noisy gongs! If pursuing ministry, let Christ designate your calling, title or assignment. In turn, the Holy Spirit will give you the appropriate gifts associated with your assignment. Do not pursue what you are not assigned. God who called you is faithful to see your assignment to completion. *"He who calls you is faithful, who also will do it"* (1 Thess. 5:24, NKJV). Only stay in your lane. If you continue to use what you have effectively, God will bring more.

Now back to the topic of contending for equal gifts. Arguments about superior anointing all stem from satan and are assigned to stagnate believers and hinder moves of God. They foster division in the Church. The best way to describe familiarity that is driven by pride and arrogance is the notion that: "We can do it better than you." The first example of this was Satan's rebellion in heaven. As the lead worshipper, he thought he had advanced enough to take over the governance of heaven like God.

Another good example is the compliant that Miriam and Aaron had about Moses. Familiarity with spiritual gifts stems from the notion that once gifted, always gifted. Arguments and assumptions of importance may lead others to think they can function or minister at a comparable level like the other. As seen with Miriam and Aaron, this is what occurred. They thought they were anointed equally as Moses.

Comparison of gifts or a sense of superiority can also breed jealously and strife in the Church. These comparisons do not produce the fruits of the Spirit, and God objects to these. With Miriam and Aaron, God responded by questioning them of their actions or slander against Moses. See the example below from Numbers 12: 1-14:

> *Miriam and Aaron began to talk against Moses because of his Cushite wife, for he had married a Cushite. Has the* LORD *spoken only through Moses?" they asked. "Hasn't he also spoken through us?" And the* LORD *heard this.*

*Now Moses was a very humble man, humbler than anyone else on the face of the earth.*

*At once the LORD said to Moses, Aaron and Miriam, "Come out to the tent of meeting, all three of you." So, the three of them went out. Then the LORD came down in a pillar of cloud; he stood at the entrance to the tent and summoned Aaron and Miriam. When the two of them stepped forward, he said, "Listen to my words: When there is a prophet among you, I, the LORD, reveal myself to them in visions, I speak to them in dreams. But this is not true of my servant Moses; he is faithful in all my house. With him I speak face to face, clearly and not in riddles; he sees the form of the LORD. Why then were you not afraid to speak against my servant Moses?"*

*The anger of the LORD burned against them, and he left them. When the cloud lifted from above the tent, Miriam's skin was leprous it became as white as snow. Aaron turned toward her and saw that she had a defiling skin disease and he said to Moses, "Please, my lord, I ask you not to hold against us the sin we have so foolishly committed. Do not let her be like a stillborn infant coming from its mother's womb with its flesh half eaten away."*

*So, Moses cried out to the LORD, "Please, God, heal her!" The LORD replied to Moses, "If her father had spit in her face, would she not have been in disgrace for seven days? Confine her outside the camp for seven days; after that she can be brought back." (NIV).*

I love this story. It not only speaks to the respect of the anointing and office each believer is given, but it also speaks to God's protective defense on behalf of Moses. Moses had no idea that Miriam and

Aaron were complaining about him, but God heard the slander and intervened even in the absence of Moses. This is perfect example of God's defense for us in our absence even when we are not aware that we are being slandered or offended. It brings more meaning to vengeance belonging to God. Our Lord fights in our absence! So, we should never worry about wanting to retaliate or explain ourselves about an adverse issue.

Miriam and Aaron were familiar with the prophetic gift, but they did not spend as much time in the tabernacle as Moses did, although Aaron was a priest. God is more interested in intimacy. The reason why Adam and Eve got immediately naked and exposed after eating the forbidden fruit is because the bond of intimacy between them and God was broken by their actions. Remember, Adam and Eve spoke and walked with God regularly prior to that. The other profound example is that of Miriam and Aaron. Instigated by Miriam, they both felt that they are equally as anointed as Moses and could also lead just as well as Moses. I believe Miriam and Aaron forgot that anointing and intimacy with God are two separate things. The two of them may have been anointed and gifted with prophesy, but they lacked intimacy with God.

I conclude this chapter by providing another good example of why we should not covet, compare, or assume one another's gifts and anticipate similar outcomes. It is the story of the seven sons of Sceva who thought they were as equally anointed as Paul. I know the story is self-explanatory, and it drives the point home.

> *Now God worked unusual miracles by the hands of Paul, so that even handkerchiefs or aprons were brought from his body to the sick, and the diseases left them and the evil spirits went out of them. Then some of the itinerant Jewish exorcists took it upon themselves to call the name of the Lord Jesus over those who had evil spirits, saying, "We exorcise you by the Jesus whom*

*Paul preaches." Also there were seven sons of Sceva, a Jewish chief priest, who did so.*

*And the evil spirit answered and said, "Jesus I know, and Paul I know; but who are you?" Then the man in whom the evil spirit was leaped on them, overpowered them, and prevailed against the so that they fled out of that house naked and wounded (Acts 19:11-16 NKJV).*

## Consider This

To the point that we feel that we have more to offer than others, or that we are more qualified or better, we go about obtaining a promotion or favor through malicious, manipulative actions or by stepping over others. In these instances, we will fall more quickly than we rise! Miriam became leprous immediately, if it were not for Moses' plea, her condition could have been permanent, but she still had to face the consequences of her actions by enduring leprosy for seven days outside the camp.

Remember that Moses was called and appointed by God to lead the Israelites. Aaron was called to support him. Miriam may have just tagged along because she was a relative. The issue here was familiarity with the prophetic gift. In fact, the main argument was paraphrased: "The Lord does not speak through Moses only; He also speaks through us." In other words, we are just as anointed as Moses.

Once we think we are equally anointed, we can erroneously conclude that we will get the same results. In this case, we become familiar with the anointing. Worse off we try to emulate another person's outcomes and manufacture them. The end results are works of the flesh and religious activities that are void of the Holy Spirit. A good illustration of this is with the most critical thing that God desired then and continues to require of believers in this age, which is intimacy with Him.

*Reflection:* Do you tend to compare your gifts and talents with someone else's? Have you ever complained or tended to criticize the effectiveness of someone else's gifts or position? Do you think you can always outrun or do better than someone else? Do you think your anointing is greater and better than someone else? Do you strive to get similar outcomes as the person you are comparing yourself with? Are you currently "competing" with someone in spiritual growth, ministerial office, or over spiritual gifts?

CHAPTER 7

# THE COST OF FAMILIARITY

≈

I am sure you have captured consequences of familiarity in previous chapters as you have read along. From Deuteronomy 1 we noticed that the costs of familiarity can be dire and deadly. Among them are the possibility of facing total defeat, underestimating of the Power of God, being overwhelmed by the situation, and underestimating the strength of the opponent. Let us review each area in detail.

**Underestimating the power of God.** God is very orderly and clear in His instructions. He will never lower, adjust, or compromise His standards. God's standards are the same yesterday, today and forever. So, He leaves us His children to choose. "And the Lord said, 'My Spirit will not always strive with man . . .'" (Gen. 6:3, NJKV). When we become so familiar with God that we expect Him to respond positively while our actions or attitudes are in rebellion or disobedience, then we have crossed the boundaries and reduced Him to human. With such attitudes, God leaves leave us to the reprobate mind, to face the consequences of such mindsets (Rom. 1:28). When this happens, we do what we want when we want. Flesh becomes master not the Holy Spirit. Being left to this mental state is God's Sovereign power, warning us that no man or woman can alter the course of God in rebellion.

**Underestimation of the opponent or the situation.** Overly imposed self-confidence that leads to downplaying any condition can be disastrous. Jesus Christ was very practical in His teachings. His lessons remain alive and applicable in this millennial age. He cautioned that "no man builds a house without for counting the cost!"

> *Suppose one of you wants to build a tower. Won't you first sit down and estimate the cost to see if you have enough money to complete it? For if you lay the foundation and are not able to finish it, everyone who sees it will ridicule you, saying, this person began to build and wasn't able to finish. Or suppose a king is about to go to war against another king. Won't he first sit down and consider whether he is able with ten thousand men to oppose the one coming against him with twenty thousand? (Luke 14:28-31, NJKV).*

Although gifts, talents, and skills are freely distributed, it is essential to develop them and to stay prepared for any situation.

Before venturing into war, study your opponent. Study your competitor. Development and preparation place us in a better position to research and evaluate how to address and manage a situation. Granted we would also have the upper hand because the Holy Spirit is with us, helping us, that is if we submit to Him. In 2 Timothy 4:2 it warns to be "ready in season and out of season." In our walk with God and in life in general, we should stay informed and equipped ourselves fully with what it takes to accomplish the assignments God has given us. Paul admonishes Timothy to study to show himself approved. We must do our best fully be equipped and ready for any assignment. This is what it means for "our feet to be ready with the gospel of peace."

Satan failed when it pertained to the death and resurrection of Christ. Satan was familiar with death and assumed Jesus's death was the end. But no, Christ's resurrection proved God's power. Christ's determination to see His assignment through, to bring us salvation, and Christ overcoming death made a shame of satan openly.

To strategically combat the issues of life, especially if they are adversarial, we must evaluate ourselves for what we have and what we do not have. Good combat involves studying and knowing what it takes. Failure to do that equals defeat.

**Works of the flesh.** Familiarity exerts works of the flesh out of self-confidence based on previous outcomes. A perfect example is the Egyptian magicians and their tricks while Moses petitioned for the Israelites to leave Egypt. When God released the plagues upon them through Moses, the magicians also copied Moses. However, we notice that God always out-performed the magicians. Most of the time, the magicians' tricks were temporary, and they failed to avert God's powerful plagues. This really translates to believers trying to do spiritual things in the flesh in our own might. The magicians were familiar with outcomes of their tricks. They thought that a) they could just do and b) it would just happen. When we become so fleshly driven we start functioning in without the Holy Spirit. It is as though we are trying to detect the Holy Spirit or worse yet mimic the Holy Spirit!

There is an increased need for believers to pray for discernment and be discerning in this millennial age. There is need for more fellowship and the dependence on the Holy Spirit and for each Christian to know the voice and the ways of the Holy Spirit. This will help Christians discern what is of the Holy Spirit, which will help to detect the increase of false teachers, signs and wonders in this age. It is now December 2016 and already the church is experiencing an outburst of false teachers; both tares and wheat growing in the same garden. Jesus explains this in Matthew 13: 24-30.

Discernment, discernment, discernment is key! We should be very cautious and discerning, watchful and prayerful in current times. When we work from the flesh, we reap the flesh. Fleshly results are short-term and disastrous. They normally require redoing them God's way anyway. When we submit to and work with the Holy Spirit, we reap the overflow of the Spirit.

**Missing out on God**. We miss out on greater things from God when we become familiar with God. Consider Naaman the leprous king whom after being instructed by Prophet Elijah to dip himself in the Jordan River, argued or reasoned about other fresh water rivers that were around. Naaman may have just assumed that to get clean one must wash with clean water not dirty Jordan River water. But, God works in mysterious ways, even what we think is foolishness is not close to human thoughts.

> *But Naaman became furious, and went away and said, "Indeed, I said to myself, 'He surely come out to me, and stand and call on the name of the Lord his God, and wave his hand over the place, and heal the leprosy.' Are not the Abanah and the Pharpar, the rivers of Damascus, better than all the waters of Israel? Could I not wash in them and be clean?" So, he turned and went away in a rage. And his servants came near and spoke to him, and said, have done it? How much more then, when he says to you, 'Wash, and be clean?'" So, he went down and dipped seven times in the Jordan, according to the saying of the man of God; and his flesh was restored like the flesh of a little child, and he was clean.*
>
> *And he returned to the man of God, he and all his aides, and came and stood before him; and he said, "Indeed, now I know that there is no God in all the earth, except in Israel; no therefore, please take a gift from your servant" (2 Kings 5:11-15, NJKV)*

"Our ways are not His ways neither are our thoughts His thoughts" (Isa. 55: 8-9). Naaman may have missed out on His healing. How about

Sarah reasoning that she was too old to give birth! Sarah too was familiar with the biological clock! Gideon also thought he needed much larger mighty army and that economical class mattered to be used by God. "Pardon me, my lord,' Gideon replied, 'but how can I save Israel? My clan is the weakest in Manasseh, and I am the least in my family" (Judg. 6: 16). Familiarity based on the above examples of Naaman, Sarah and Gideon is a mindset; a false belief! False belief is unbelief.

Unbelief that is a result agreeing with statistics, historic accounts, or medical science forms the worst grounds for the miraculous to occur. In fact, such mindsets defy and underestimate God's power. The best thing to do is submit to God's ways and get out His way. God may want to teach us something new, mature us expose us to other options and far better things. Whenever God wants to do a new thing, He does it exceedingly, abundantly above what we know, think, or ask.

**Hurt, pain, and betrayal from humans.** This section comes from personal life experiences. When people become so familiar with you, at times they are bound to no longer respect you, value your time, service, or commitment to them. Humans may assume your reaction and conclude that you are accepting of their conduct towards you. The toughest part is when you have invested too much into a person and receive the opposite outcome. This is how we expose ourselves to hurt, pain, betrayal, exploitation, abuse, and sufferings. Females are likely to be trapped into this, especially when longing for acceptance or affirmation.

I am a strong believer of "you treat people how to treat you." Can you recall the day you put your foot down and confronted those who took you for granted? I also believe that born again Christians can confront and address conflict respectfully and biblically without being "nasty" with one another. Have noticed thought the day you say no how quickly they may react with, "I did not know that upset you," "I thought you accepted it because you acted like it did not bother you," or even "Oh we never thought he would react like that."

The lesson here is that never let people get so familiar with you that they cross boundaries. Do you best to address something you are uncomfortable with immediately? Granted, there is still a need to ask the Holy Spirit for the right approach and timing to address the issue. Personally, I believe that it is crucial to settle conflicts and not avoid them or throw them under the rug, and that it should be done after praying and at the guidance of the Holy Spirit. Having said that, they are issues the Holy Spirit may tell you to address. There are issues He may tell you to forgo forever, and there are issues that He may ask you to address at a much later time. Obeying what the Holy Spirit tells you to do is very crucial.

**Death or destruction.** Satan comes to steal, kill, and destroy. John 10:10 says: "The thief comes only to steal, and to kill, and to destroy. I have come that they may have life, and that they may have it more abundantly" (NKJV). No matter how convincing, he may sound, it is always a camouflage. His agenda is never for the good. He may entice and lead one to think that he means well, but it is always temporary. I am learning that whenever I am driven to hurry and do something without seeking God first, it is almost always for self-gratification and never from God. Whenever we decide to exclude God and operate in our own strength, we open the door for negative outcomes. Satan's aim is the fight and destroy God's plan. Like the Israelites in Ai, they encountered defeat because they went to war in their one accord.

**Unbelief and fear.** The underlying cause of unbelief is fear, fear of the unknown and the unexpected status. Fear of the giants and unbelief in the promises of God was the attitude and reason that the ten spies hesitated in capturing Canaan, the land that God had already promised the Israelites. Fear in the unknown and unbelief in the power of God were the main factors that made the Israelites want to return to Egypt after they had been delivered from it. In fact, they told Moses that at least they ate healthier vegetables in Egypt than the desert where they were. Instead of trusting in God, they resorted to what they were familiar with, which was their past experiences in the land of Goshen.

Never allow fear and unbelief to overtake you. Overcome them instead. These two are very damaging to our Christian walk and are influenced demonically. God always has something greater when He directs you to do something differently or to move or take a contrary step. The just shall live by faith; that is the scripture. Refuse to return to what God has delivered you from. Trust God to lead you to the unfamiliar territory. God will never leave you there alone. He will never put you to shame.

**Don't rock the boat.** Familiarity can result in maintaining the status quo because of being familiar and comfortable with the current condition they are in. Being comfortable is not bad, but being comfortable when there's more that God can still do through you is concerning. Allow God to place the period in your destiny. Do not self-impose and settle where you are in life because you are familiar with the environment, the people around you, friends or family, or with the processes and produces. A good parent or mentor will always push you farther with the aim of making you better and greater. Keep off the comfort zone. There is a familiar saying that "if it aint broken, don't fix it," but to advance to greater things, it may require leaving what's not broken alone and moving on to something newer and better.

**Think alike mentality.** This is the effect of mob-mentality. In the Ai defeat, people agreed to war despite direction not to. The problem with mob-mentality is that the hysteria takes over logic and reasoning. In group settings, most of the campaigning and advocacy can take place to convict recruit more candidates, to gain support. The notion being that there is power in numbers. Often, it is great to have this if going after God's will, if not, the results lead to destruction. In the mix of unhealthy noise, we also miss out on hearing from God. Bad company spoils. In the Bible, several accounts of rebellion are noted to have been started by just a few people, then many were influenced. You can read this starting with Eve being deceived and Korah leading the rebellion against Moses and Aaron. Fast forward to the New Testament, and you'll see it where the Pharisees and Sadducees incite people against Jesus and later with Apostle Paul and others. Mob-mentality is likely the reason that the whole army went against God to attack Ai. So far, I'm learning that God rarely talks directly to a collective group of people, He normally talks to one person, and then that messenger relays the message.

# SECTION II
# COMBATING FAMILIARITY

# CHAPTER 8

# DO YOUR HOMEWORK—SPY

≈

As I reflect on my life, I have identified multiple areas in the past that I had the opportunity to change the outcome or course of direction if I had only done my homework. As much as we need to rely on God for guidance, I believe there are aspects of our walk that God desires for us to take the initiative and act on as part of His maturing process for us. God loves to make us responsible and keep us knowledgeable through diverse experiences, exposures, and training.

Part of this training is to know what you are getting into. As for the Israelites, since God was training them to go to war, His servants often sent spies to scout their opponents. This was done to ascertain the manpower and ammunition required for the war. I call this "spying." In fact, the original heading for this chapter was "Become a Spy." Have you wondered why, although Joshua and Caleb had full access of God's protective power and glory, they still sent spies to scout the territories (lands) they were about to possess? (See Josh. 6:1-27.)

Another reason why we should spy and not just assume is so that you can identify the value of what you are about to venture into. "Is it worth it?" is the question to ask. Spy by researching where you are going, what you want to venture into, and what your opponents are doing. Since they were treading on new territories, they sent spies scout the lands to determine whether it is worth the fight. They wanted to see what they could benefit from the land and whether it would be for short-term gain, or long-term generational gain.

Spy by seeking counsel from trusted people around you. You will know these people by the revelation of the Holy Spirit and by their fruits (character, attitude, and lifestyle). *"Without counsel, plans go awry, but in the multitude of counselors they are established"* (Prov. 15:22, NJKV). *"For lack of guidance a nation falls, but victory is won through many advisers"* (Prov. 11:14, NIV).

## *Consider This*

The most important thing we need to evaluate is whether we want to grow spiritually and whether we have submitted to God's leadership in maturing us. With that commitment comes the responsibility to do our part in what God assigns us to do.

Proverbs 25:2 states: *"It is the glory of God to conceal a thing: but the honor of kings is to search out a matter"* (KJV). As an informed believer, you have strategies and know who and what you are dealing with. This also includes being strategic in prayer. We can avoid pitfalls and repeated cycles of defeat. If venturing into a new business, marriage, career, house, etc., spy using the examples above and acquire information to make the right choices. After one victorious outcome, you will gain faith and are ready to take on the next venture! Bring it on! *"This is the confidence we have in approaching God: that if we ask anything per His will, He hears us"* (1 John 5:14, NKJV). Do not just take risks; take calculated God ordained risks. They always produce very fruitful outcomes. No more Christian causalities! Do your part, do your homework, and be a spy.

*Reflection:* If you look back in your life, are there areas that were compromised due to your failure to research or do your homework? The key question to answer is why you failed to do the homework. The answer to that question may help evaluate what area in your life needs maturity.

# CHAPTER 9

# DISCERN THE ADVICE YOU RECEIVE

≈

King Jehoshaphat in 2 Chronicles 18 and 20 provides a very good example of walking in discernment and knowing the voice God. Because of his dedication and commitment to God, King Jehoshaphat knew God's voice well enough to disguise it from deceptive voices. He managed to do this even among the experts who currently, most could have settled for just because they were prophets. See the king's story below:

> But Jehoshaphat asked, "Is there no longer a prophet of the Lord here whom we can inquire of? The king of Israel answered Jehoshaphat, "There is still one prophet through whom we can inquire of the Lord, but I hate him because he never prophesies anything good about me, but always bad. He is Micaiah son of Imlah." The king should not say such a thing," Jehoshaphat replied. So, the king of Israel called one of his officials and said, "Bring Micaiah son of Imlah at once" (2 Chron. 18:6-8, NIV).

The background of the above scriptures is the account of King Jehoshaphat agreeing to partner with another king to go to war. It is also important to note that this other king, Ahab, was not God-fearing like King Jehoshaphat. So, Jehoshaphat demanded that an inquiry be made of God whether it was God's will to go and/or whether victory was guaranteed if Jehoshaphat joined in war. I hope you have noticed a pattern in the scriptures outlined in the book so far that it was common for the Israelites to seek God's direction through prophets or directly in prayer if they were about to launch into war pursue a new thing.

The caution in 2 Chronicles 18:6-8 is that 400 prophets approved moving forth with going to war, but despite the huge number of collective prophesy, saying: "All the other prophets were prophesying the same thing: 'Attack Ramoth Gilead and be victorious,' they said, 'for the Lord will give it into the king's hand'" (2 Chron. 18:11, NIV). However, Jehoshaphat was discerning enough to inquire still that a "true prophet" be contacted. At this request, king Ahab summoned Micaiah the prophet who prophesied defeat and king Ahab's death if they pursued the war.

The reason why it was important for King Jehoshaphat to be very discerning in this matter is because of this: "So now the Lord has put a deceiving spirit in the mouths of these prophets of yours. The Lord has decreed disaster for you" (2 Chron. 18:22, NIV). The deceptive spirit here was satan. Satan entered the four hundred prophets to prophesy falsely to both kings; but it took Jehoshaphat's discernment to know that that prophesy was not from God. Apostle Paul in his letter to the Corinthians warned against such enticement and false prophets or teachers. He says in 2 Corinthians 11:14-15: "And no wonder, for Satan himself masquerades as an angel of light. It is not surprising, then, if his servants also masquerade as servants of righteousness. Their end will be what their actions deserve" (NIV). The Apostle Peter also warns in 1 Peter 5:8, "We should be sober, be vigilant; because your adversary the devil, as a roaring lion, walks about, seeking whom he may devour" (KJV).

# Consider This

Being sober means being clear-headed, alert, intuitive, discerning, and in the context of this chapter being aware of your surroundings as well as, most importantly, being able to distinguish the voice of God from the voice of satan. This requires being filled with the Spirit of Discernment according to Isaiah 11:2. In addition to being filled with the Holy Spirit; maturing in the Holy Spirit requires continuous fellowship and interaction with Him. This can be done through prayer and cultivating intimacy with the Holy Spirit as well as knowing His voice and obeying what He says.

Staying vigilant requires taking a stand and being bold to confront larger volumes of oppositions, taking the risk to be the sole person that will question, and standing for what is right. Jehoshaphat stood against the counsel of 400 prophets. Even after the 400 had prophesied, Jehoshaphat asked King Ahab, "Is there no longer a prophet of the Lord here whom we can inquire of?" The key point here being the words "prophet of the Lord." This makes you wonder and even concluded that the 400 prophets were not appointed by God. In the Old Testament, there are multiple accounts of kings worshiping other gods and having prophets of those god's prophesy to the kings.

King Jehoshaphat's stance against many false prophets confirms that one person can alter destiny. That God does not move in numbers. This mirrors the story of Moses and the twelve spies in Numbers chapter 13. Of the twelve, only two returned with good news, the rest had contrary news.

Many in this prophetic age could have succumbed to the false prophesy of the 400 prophets just because of the volume. In fact, in this age we could have hastily said that these were 400 confirmations that we should proceed but Jehoshaphat had the discerning Spirit to inquire.

Relying solely on the revelation of others is not safe. Do not depend fully or live totally on the revelation of others. The most tangible and impactful revelations are the ones God gives you personally. Foster intimacy with the Holy Spirit then obey and do what He tells you. You will be amazed at how much He will show you. This is the bread of life! The revelations from others may confirm what God already told you or expound, so don't brush them off either.

*Reflection:* Are there areas of your life that have negative outcomes due to receiving false counsel? Do you exercise discernment or seek God in prayer before implementing any counsel? Do you tend to believe and act on every prophesy you receive? "*Do not despise prophecies, but test everything; hold fast what is good*" (1 Thess. 5:20-21 NJKV).

CHAPTER 10

# WATCH YOUR COMPANY

≈

"A little leaven leavens the whole lump" (Gal. 5:9, NKJV). I have never valued the importance of being mindful of who you are connected to or who you associate with when pursuing destiny like I am now. I realized this back in 2014 when God had started shifting me towards my identity and destiny.

Familiarity with God can be very common among us Christians, especially if we were brought up in church or have been saved for a while. We can easily assume that "we have arrived" and therefore know God inside and out. With such attitudes, we can easily compromise on little things, and slowly but surely these things can grow and pull us away from our destinies. The little leaven in my definition would be those "nice things" that are in themselves not sinful or harmful. They may sound spiritual, but they are non-scriptural, and they make us feel good or feel religious. These may present themselves as ideas, doctrines, rituals, or practices that provide us sense of godliness but that are utterly void of God or the Holy Spirit.

If applied to humans, these would include associations or acquaintances who know God but whose lifestyles or characters are far from the God's. Such people normally have strong religious spirits, which emphasize works rather than the Holy Spirit. Commonly, you may observe the absence of the fruits of the Spirit in them. Galatians 5:22-23 states: "But the fruit of the Spirit is love, joy, peace, longsuffering, kindness, goodness, faithfulness, gentleness, self-control. Against such there is no law." This is why Apostle Paul warned: "Do not be unequally yoked together with unbelievers. For what fellowship has righteousness with lawlessness? And what communion has light with darkness?" (2 Cor. 6:14, NJKV).

## Consider This

Surrounding yourself with the wrong kind of company can lead to compromise and dire outcomes. King Jehoshaphat missed dying narrowly when he ignored the Lord's counsel and proceeded with the king Ahab's advice. "So, it was, when the captains of the chariots saw Jehoshaphat, that they said, 'It is the king of Israel.' Therefore, they surrounded him to attack; but Jehoshaphat cried out, and the Lord helped him; and God moved them to depart from him" (2 Chron. 18:31, NJKV).

In 2 Chronicles 19: 1-3, we see the admonition King Jehoshaphat was given-*Then Jehoshaphat the king of Judah returned safely to his house in Jerusalem. And Jehu the son of Hanani the seer went out to meet him, and said to King Jehoshaphat, "Should you help the wicked and love those who hate the Lord? Therefore, the wrath of the Lord is upon you. Nevertheless, good things are found in you, in that you have removed the wooden images from the land, and have prepared your heart to seek God (NJKV).*

From the paragraphs above, we notice the dire consequences of bad company and wrong advices as well as the redeeming grace of God's mercy and grace to forgive and restore.

*Reflection:* Has bad company made you disobey God? Are you ready to denounce and cut off the bad company? Are you open to repenting and asking God for forgiveness and restoration?

CHAPTER 11

# INQUIRE OF THE LORD

≈

Assumptions, specifically with God, humans, and other things, can leave us deprived of better outcomes. More now than ever before, there is an urgency to solely depend on the Holy Spirit and rely on Him for direction.

From personal experience with God, I am learning that God rarely repeats His ways to bring us victory or breakthrough. God tends to use various means of doing this, and His timing may also vary. It is very important that we seek His guidance for every area of our lives. This also involves asking for God's guidance in ministry. While ministering, one may assume that the Holy Spirit will do this and that just as He normally does or just like He moved in the first service or session, but God moves differently most of the time. This requires that we call on Him and depend on Him always.

We should inquire of the Lord before we venture into new missions concerning our destinies and for every aspect of our lives. As the first born in my family, I noticed something "weird" with my siblings as they grew older. At 25 years, old, I realized that I could not raise all four siblings the same way. They each had different personalities and responded to my advice differently. Initially, I used to be frustrated when they could not follow my direction, until one evening while standing in my living room the Holy Spirit just ministered to me saying: "Pauline each child is different, and you must also approach the boys differently than you approach your sisters." This has made a big difference in my life to date.

# Consider This

God has different strategies for every encounter. We would be missing out on Him if we relied on previous encounters for the same outcomes. The key scriptures of this book highlight the impact of failing to inquire of the Lord due to familiarity. The Israelites failure in Ai was because they failed to inquire from God.

King Jehoshaphat's account, though encouraging, is also revealing in that, although he inquired of the Lord, Jehoshaphat ignored Prophet Micaiah's prophesy and joined king Ahab for war. The key lesson here is to obey God's directives and the Holy Spirit one we have inquired from Him.

Finally, there are consequences of inquiring from alternative sources. This can mean seeking man's advice verses God's or resorting to occult and divination for direction. Doing this for a born-again believer is really opening doors for demonic operations in addition to being a sin before God. We learn this from King Saul' story. The scriptures are quite self-explanatory: *"So, Saul died for his unfaithfulness which he had committed against the Lord, because he did not keep the word of the Lord, and because he consulted a medium for guidance. But he did not inquire of the Lord; therefore, He killed him, and turned the kingdom over to David the son of Jesse" (1 Chron. 10:14, NJKV).*

Nevertheless, when we inquire from the Lord, He hears and responds. This is the assurance we have with our loving God that He hears our cries and responds to the prayers of His children. This is contrary to the Ai incident when we see the tribe of Gad call on God as they war towards their destiny to obtain their promised land: "*And they were helped against them, and the Hagrites were delivered into their hand, and all who were with them, for they cried out to God in the battle. He heeded their prayer, because they put their trust in Him*" (1 Chron. 5:20, NJKV).

*Reflection:* Are there areas in your life or ministry that things could have gone differently had you inquired of the Lord? Are you in constant surrender and submission to God; that He may do something better or greater or do you ignore the asking and move in your plans? Do you habitually seek first God's Kingdom that everything else may be added to you?

# CHAPTER 12

# GOD WILL PROVIDE THE WINNING STRATEGY

≈

Have you ever reached your wit's end trying to solve a problem, especially after exhausting resources and finding no solution from friends or even from those you trust? If you are the one who is always sought out as the problem solver, failure to provide a resolution can be frustrating. Today, I would like to provide you an alternative to your frustration. Though simplistic by nature, this solution is the most powerful and guaranteed step in dealing with the unsolvable. The solution is "give the issue to God."

Nothing is impossible with God, according to Jeremiah 32:17, which states: *"Ah, Lord God! Behold, You have made the heavens and the earth by Your great power and outstretched arm. There is nothing too hard for You (NKJV).* Further in the New Statements confirms this attribute of God in Matthew 19:26b, "with God all things are possible" (NJKV). God never fails. It is quite encouraging when we lean or let God fight on our behalf strategies are sure to succeed. Here are the reasons why.

**God desires to take the issues off ourselves and give them to Him.** This is such a caring attribute of God as our Father. He calls on those who are heavily laden to come to Him for rest. The burden in this context is the problem you cannot solve or issue you need breakthrough in.

*"Come to me, all you who are weary and burdened, and I will give you rest. Take my yoke upon you and learn from me, for I am gentle and humble in heart, and you will find rest for your souls. For my yoke is easy and my burden is light "(Matthew 11:28–30, NKJV).* Moreover, God desires that are freed from anything that would cause us anxiety. He wants us to trust Him to solve all issues that is why He directs us to cast all our care upon Him, for He cares for us. (See 1 Peter 5:7.)

**God is mindful of each of us in His strategic plans for us.** As our creator, God knows our ins and outs. In fact, He says He searches our hearts and souls in addition to knowing our frailties and strengths. It as though God conducts a thorough assessment of us before launching us into something. He is very mindful of our success in what He had ordained for us. Consider how he protected the Israelites as they journeyed in the desert. At start of their journey there was a short cut that would involve walking across the land of the Philistines. *"So, God led the people around by way of the wilderness of the Red Sea. And the children of Israel went up in orderly ranks out of the land of Egypt" (Exodus 13:18, NKJV).* God may lead us the alternate way or even take a detour, but while doing this, know that He is protecting us, leading us through the safer ways. Despite the detour, God will still lead us to the desired outcome. Historically, God's outcome exceeds what we predict or expect. So just follow His direction knowing you are headed for more than what you thought or expected.

**God strategies may not make sense to human minds.** If God were human, then His plans would be logical and sensible to us, but God is not a human. He does not think like we do, no matter how intelligent we are. *"For my thoughts are not your thoughts, neither are your ways my ways, declares the Lord" (Isaiah 55:8, NJKV).* However, once God gives us (man) the solution, we always are left in awe wondering how smart He was in bringing us to that conclusion. God shows this aspect of Him in the following verse in Isaiah 55:9: *"For as the heavens are higher than the earth, so are My ways higher than your ways, And My thoughts than your thoughts" (NKJV).* Examples of God's non-conventional ways of strategies include that of army of Israel matching around a city to bring the city down as shown in Joshua chapter 6. Joshua obeyed and followed the none conventional strategy to march around Jericho.

**What man perceives as simple is very effective in God's strategies.** With God, it does not matter what He uses. In fact, God has historically used very simple things, never complex and detailed initiatives, all very simple. With David, it was rocks not heavy-duty ammunition. With Naaman the king, it was dipping himself in water seven times, and with Noah, it was the boat. God repeatedly asked the Israelites to praise and worship Him. Whenever these were done, Israel's enemies were at times confused. The enemies either ran away from the battlefield or fought amongst themselves. With Jael, she used a peg and a hammer to kill the adversarial king, and with Gideon, a down-sized army.

Once you have submitted to God, trust what God tells you to do and just follow. No matter how illogical the instructions may sound, commit to following without questioning "why?" By nature, the solution God will provide you will confound the wise! But God chose the foolish things of the world to shame the wise; God chose the weak things of the world to shame the strong. (See 1 Corinthians 1:27.)

**God's strategies may involve causing your adversary or condition to work in your favor.** In many occasions as Israelites walked through the desert to acquire new land, God imposed fear in the nations based on the testimony of His works in leading them out of Egypt. Some nations even feared before the Israelites took over their cities. See Rahab's confession to the two spies. Here is the account from Joshua 2:8-11:

> *Now before they lay down, she came up to them on the roof, and said to the men: "I know that the Lord has given you the land, that the terror of you has fallen on us, and that all inhabitants of the land are fainthearted because of you. For we have heard how the Lord dried up the water of the Red Sea for you when you came*

*out of Egypt, and what you did to the two kings of the Amorites who were on the other side of the Jordan, Sihon and Og, whom you utterly destroyed. And as soon as we heard these things, our hearts melted; neither did there remain any more courage in anyone because of you, for the Lord your God, He is God in heaven above and on earth beneath (NKJV).*

If you read further in Joshua chapter 9, some tribes resulted to pretentious behaviors just to submit to the Israelites. See the accounts of the Gibeonite's deception in Joshua 9:3-22. In verse 24 of the same chapter, the Gibeonite's, surrender to Joshua. They answered Joshua, "Truly the Lord has delivered the land into our hands, for indeed all the inhabitants of the country are fainthearted because of us" (NKJV).

Be prepared for your adversaries or the negative situation to work on your behalf because all things work together for good to them that love God, to them who are the called according to his purpose. (See Rom. 8:28.)

**God takes lead in coordinating the strategies.** If you study God's war strategies under David's or Joshua's leadership, God always gave the go-ahead or redirected them whenever they inquired to pursue their enemies in war. For the most part God would orchestrate these plans by directing them on how they should coordinate their armies then leave them to utilize their common sense to win. God coordinated the winning strategy. Likewise, God may give us all the tools and people to help solve the problem. Be assured that once God has spoken He does so because His words must perform what He says! His word is sure, and likewise His strategies never fail. It is up to us to recognize the tools we have been given and utilize them to our advantage. When unsure, ask God to open your eyes to see what He has assigned. (See 2 Kings 2:17.)

**At times God fights by creating utter confusion on any challenge to our breakthrough.** I love it. A perfect example is what happened to the Egyptian army when it pursued the Israelites in the Red Sea. All it took was God to look down. Exodus 14:23-25 says: "The Egyptians pursued with all the horses of Pharaoh, his chariots, and his horsemen and they went into the middle of the sea after them. In the morning watch, the Lord looked down on the Egyptian camp through the pillar of fire and cloud, and he threw the Egyptian camp into confusion. He made the wheels of their chariots wobble so that they drove them with difficulty. The Egyptians said, 'Let's flee from Israel because the Lord is fighting for them and against us.'" When I read that God looked down through the cloud, and the wheels of the Egyptian chariots started to disassemble, I thought Hallelujah! The Egyptians themselves warned "let's go back, their God is fighting for them." God's mighty power is so profound that our adversary must testify and depart when God's fights for us.

When faced with challenges, focus on God not the challenge. God may just look down and bring confusion to the weapons or means that satan is utilizing against you. In fact, this is further attested in Isaiah 54:16-17:

> *See, it is I who created the blacksmith who fans the coals into flame and forges a weapon fit for its work and it is I who have created the destroyer to wreak havoc; no weapon forged against you will prevail, and you will refute every tongue that accuses you. This is the heritage of the servants of the Lord, and this is their vindication from me, "declares the Lord. (NIV).*

Since God created the weapons that would be used and the user of those weapons, God can frustrate both the weapons and the user of those weapons on your behalf!

**At times God fights in silence.** The best assurance I can give on God's silence is that God is the Alpha and Omega. He sees the end from the beginning. So, when He seems quiet because you have not seen a resolution to your problem yet, most likely it is because God is protecting you from something or preserving the resolution for the right time. God works best in our deserts and night hours. Recall the armies that went against the Israelites. At night confusion arose. Some were blinded so that they fought each other. When the Israelites woke up the next day, the enemies were dead and scattered. God did the same with Egyptians. The Israelites crossed over in terror of ambush at night, but when daylight came, they saw dead bodies floating ashore! When waiting for an answer from God, focus not on the delay. Just trust that God is up to something great!

**At times, God will stir up those in higher positions to favor you.** God works in mysterious ways. He may cause those in authority to favor and act on your behalf to bring a solution. This may be a boss, an employer, or your pastor. With Abraham, God used Abimelech to bless him with wealth. (See Genesis 20:18.) Mortdecai's' salvation and promotion came through a disturbing dream that the king had. (See Esther 6.)

Watch out for those opportunities. God may stir up executives, leaders and people in authority to bless you. Expand your horizon and stay open to the diversified ways God may use to strategize the success of your desired outcomes. Continue to trust in the Lord with ALL your heart and lean not in your understanding, in all your ways acknowledge Him and He will make straight your paths. Relax, let God handle it. He is very good at both vengeance and recompense. *God will provide the winning strategy!*

# CHAPTER 13

# REST IN THE LORD—LET GOD HAVE HIS WAY

≈

Philippians 4:7 states: *"And the peace of God, which transcends all understanding, will guard your hearts and your minds in Christ Jesus"* *(NJKV).*

With time, familiarity may cause us to function on autopilot where we program ourselves to react or manage things a certain way just because that is how we have always handled things to gain the outcomes we have achieved. This attitude causes us to deepen our efforts and engage our personal wills to get the desired outcomes. This attitude also can cause us to constantly gear towards "works," that is what we can do in our human power to resolve the issue instead of relying or seeking the Lord's direction.

Positive results may not necessarily be God's will. When we rely on our efforts, we may become complacent and neglect seeking God. Moreover, we may end up being burnt-out, anxious, tired, and frustrated when we press in our own efforts for breakthrough. Yet, I have come to learn that God does more for us and through us when we are in a position of rest.

Rest is a position of letting go and allowing God to have His way in the situation. It is a place of total surrender, submitting all to God. Rest involves allowing the mind, body, emotions, and soul to just be. The scripture, "be still and know that I am God," comes to mind. More and more I am learning the importance of rest and resting in the Lord. I have come to experience and believe that God does more with us and shows us more of Him when we are in a place of rest. It is my hope that you can come to a position of rest, where rest becomes a lifestyle and an environment that keeps you in constant fellowship with God and His people.

First, this rest comes through redemption and being accepted as God's children and partakers of Christ in His place of rest. Based on ongoing experience with the Holy Spirit, the place of rest is fully steered and brought about by the wonderful Holy Spirit. He started by endowing me with the Spirit of Joy. I describe it as an unexplained "joyous high" where my mind, emotions, and body have less tolerance for offenses. My mind could be very upset, yet my heart would be very still and joyous and within a short period, the offense would lift off completely, and I would be fully joyful again.

This rest also comes by experiencing the inner rest and healing from the Lord. As God's children, to experience His fullness, we must empty ourselves of what is unclean, embrace what is clean, and be filled with what is clean. Emptying ourselves of our human efforts and submitting to the Holy Spirit are essential to be filled with more of Him. 2 Timothy 2:20-21 says: "*But in a great house there are not only vessels of gold and silver, but also of wood and clay, some for honor and some for dishonor. Therefore, if anyone cleanses himself from the latter, he will be a vessel for honor, sanctified and useful for the Master, prepared for every good work*" (NKJV).

This rest comes by forgiving the unforgivable, letting go of past hurts and pains, letting go of any resentment of bitterness, jealously, and anything that is secret that continues to wound or hurt. You rest by letting go. Next, rest can come through assurance in His promises. I am an avid reader of the Bible, but I recall a day in November 2015 when the verse came alive. *"Be anxious for nothing, but in everything by prayer and supplication, with thanksgiving, let your requests be made known to God; and the peace of God, which surpasses all understanding, will guard your hearts and minds through Christ Jesus" (Phil. 4:6-7, NJKV).* Literally, from that moment it is as though my mind fights and refuses to entertain anxiety. When the thoughts of "what if" and "what about" and "how" start, my mind switches to this scripture. At times, it is as though the Holy Spirit is telling me to "knock it off" with reminders, such as "What is faith then? You pray Pauline, don't you?" "Yes, Holy Spirit," I would answer. You too can rest from anxieties and cares. Leave the burden at the cross, even Christ Himself now seated at the right hand of God is free of burdens. If He lives in us, let us also release every burden to Him.

Come to rest by setting your minds on Jesus. *"Set your mind on things that are above not on earthly things, Col. 3:2, NIV.* If you can reflect and see yourself seated at the right handoff God with Jesus. We are co-heirs with Him; His Kingdom is in us. The greatest battle and war is in our minds. As God's children, we are embraced in His love, and our thoughts and minds are therefore set to the principles and laws of the Kingdom that we are in, which is the God's Kingdom. By having the mind of Christ, we will see and think as God sees, from God's perspective. When this happens, we experience peace, rest comes, and our minds are freed. We can also come to rest in the assurance of God's promises for us by allowing our thoughts to be transformed. This involves filling our minds with things that are good and that deserve praise, things that are true, noble, right, pure, lovely, and honorable according to Philippians 4:8. I have discovered that I can and ALL OF US can still come to a place of rest in Christ Jesus while still alive!

This rest also comes through peace in the Spirit. I've come to experience this rest by receiving the gift of peace. The peace that Christ left with us, "My peace I give you." I really cannot describe it other than being in a place of stillness. So still, I can touch the thin transparent stillness of this peace. It is a peace that surpasses human understanding. It sure is!

As you let go and surrender all to God, rest in the assurance of Gods promises for you. Rest in faith and hope that God, who said it, will be sure to perform interest in prayer and the studying of His Word. Rest by stopping the works, be delivered from the religious spirit of "I have to do to please God." Rest in the assurance of your identity in Christ, accepting that God loves you. Rest in being the you in God, staying open and embracing God's love for you, and embracing what He has for you.

Surrender and welcome the peace of the Holy Spirit. Rest by praying, cast your cares to God for He cares for you. Rest by praising God in thanksgiving. Rest by singing. When anxiety, fear, doubt or questions arise, rest in the assurance of God as our all in all. Rest in God our Papa. Sit on His lap and enjoy His embrace and warmth. He is our affirmation. He alone validates us. He is our firm foundation. We are edified and assured by Him. He is our supporter and cheerleader, our fortress in whom we are firmly grounded. In His rest, we stand unshakeable.

This rest is the place of experiencing God's fullness, His continuous presence, His fellowship. It is the experience of the stillness of God. This rest can be found in the Kingdom of God, which is righteousness, peace, and joy in the Holy Spirit. We can experience rest on earth while still alive.

If you would like to surrender all to God and are ready to embrace this rest, say this prayer with me.

> *Father in the Name of Jesus, I thank you that you care for me and desire that enjoy my life in you. I release every area of unforgiveness, bitterness, and resentment and ask for your forgiveness. I forgive those who have offended me. I repent of my self-effort and unbelief. With*

*my hand on my heart, I ask the Holy Spirit to expose any hidden wounds and bring healing permanently. With hands on my heads, In the name of Jesus and by the Blood of Jesus I command very brain cell, conscious and subconscious mind cleansed and healed. I declare that my body, our homes, my families and my generations are healed and restored. I now we embrace this new season of rest. I embrace God's love. I receive the in filling of the Holy Spirit and ask that every gift be activated. I receive impartations towards living in the fullness of your destinies. I receive the Spirit of God, the Spirit of wisdom, counsel, revelation, discernment, power, glory, and fire, the wind of the Holy Spirit and fullness of the Spirit. I embrace the future, with more, dreams, visions, and purpose but from a place of rest in Jesus Name, Amen.*

# CHAPTER 14

# GOD DOES MORE WHEN
# WE ARE FLEXIBLE

≈

The world is becoming smaller given the enhancing new technology that has simplified communication and forced us to let go of traditions and rigidity and adapt to stay with the times. This adaptability is also required in our walk as believers. Among the key strategies for success in spiritual growth, life, or ministry is being flexible and accommodating of everything God wants to do with and in us.

If we are true to ourselves and claim total loyalty or commitment to God, then we must submit to God as the potter and we as the clay. With this understanding, we must submit to the stretching, molding, and shaping of the Lord. We must remain flexible to the shape and vessel God wants to make us.

> *The word which came to Jeremiah from the LORD saying, Arise and go down to the potter's house, and there I will announce My words to you." Then I went down to the potter's house, and there he was, making something on the wheel. But the vessel that he was making of clay was spoiled in the hand of the potter; so, he remade it into another vessel, as it pleased the potter to make. Then the word of the LORD came to me saying, "Can I not, O house*

> *of Israel, deal with you as this potter does?" declares the*
> LORD. *"Behold, like the clay in the potter's hand, so are*
> *you in My hand, O house of Israel. (Jer. 18: 1-6, NASB).*

Additionally, I have realized that flexibility and obedience are key to increase in the knowledge and fullness of God. (See Isaiah 64:8.) Clay is flexible. In fact, its consistency has some viscosity that makes in pliable, conformable and shapeable to whatever thing the Potter wants. The outcome is normally something beautiful; often a vessel to contain something of value or a decorative, pleasant, and ready for good use.

Flexibility is an attitude of total surrender that occurs when we submit to God as our potter, to conform and shape us into what He wants us to be. Once conformable, God in turn uses various ways including tests, adversity, chastening, and blessings to mold us into His image. Do not be quick to want to cop-out of an adversity or test because it could be that God is using that situation to mold and shape you. Instead, remain open and flexible. Let His hands work on you, that you may be shaped and molded to a usable vessel. This is our God. Embrace the freedom in Christ. Our walk as Christians is no longer by works, or on our own. Our walk rather is by faith, and with the Holy Spirit.

Familiarity is being adaptable and obedient to the unconventional ways that God may use to direct you. Throughout the Bible we see that God rarely operated the same way although similar goals were always achieved. To cure leprosy, the directions were to dip in dirty water seven times, but to the other lepers in the New Testament, Jesus tells him to go show himself to the priest. Miriam on the other hand was healed after sitting out the main gate for seven days. In wars, God fought battles for the Israelites by blinding their opponents, by directing a match around a wall, by allowing the sun to stand still by having Moses's hand held up as the army fought and by having the red sea swallow opponents in their pursuit.

Flexibility with God produces more! When we are hung up on our ways, we seem to only see the results and outcomes from our perspective. Yet God does more. Naaman's story comes to mind. I am not sure how old he was but his skin was restored to a baby's skin, not a grown man's skin. Sarah's faith and being open to God's unwavering word produced a power nation that exists to date—Israel. If we approach God without constraints and give Him the free flow to take over our agenda and plans, God is true to His Word when He says He does exceedingly above all we think or know. I have experienced God do and show me more whenever I submitted to change my own plans and allowed Him to direct my day.

By staying flexible, we can be stretched, bended, twisted, pruned, plucked, chastened, and molded to the perfect shape God wants us to be. In all, we are created in His image, and all these are to bring us the fullness of that image. After all, our thoughts are His not ours. God knows best. It would behoove us to stay comfortable, flexible, and open to what He is doing with and in us.

## *Consider This*

The key lesson that I have learned with God is that He rarely directs us to do the same thing. This way we should not assume or take for granted that He will direct us or move in the same manner He moved before. There is still a need to depend on God and ask for His direction. There remains a need to submit and obey the directives He gives. There remains a need to trust and walk by faith, understanding that regardless of how unconventional God's instructions are, God's Word will not be in void. He will still do what He sent His Word to do. Count on God to show up.

*Reflection:* Can you identity areas that you may have missed God because you expected Him to move a certain way? Do you have tendencies to be rigid or have religious routines, personal principles, or ways of doing things?

# CHAPTER 15

# THE POWER OF THANKSGIVING AND PRAISE FOR BREAKTHROUGH

≈

As I conclude the subject on familiarity, I cannot help but reflect on the power of praise, worship, and thanksgiving as potent weapons to be engaged in while waiting for breakthrough. Praise, worship, and thanksgiving are common strategies used entirely in the Bible, and they brought tremendous victories.

We find evidence of this in several accounts in scripture, but the three stand out for me. First are of Paul and Silas praising God while imprisoned and God moving through an earthquake, shaking the chains, and setting them free. The next story is of Joshua and the army marching around the Jericho wall. On the seventh day, the Lord directed that the army march seven times, then trumpets be blown with the priests and worshippers leading the army. When praise and worship preceded, the walls of Jericho came down and Israelites captured the city. The third story is King Jehoshaphat's account in 2 Chronicles 20. This story is when the Moabites and Ammonites with some of the Meunites decided to wage war over Israel.

The lesson from this decision is that satan likes to wage war against the righteous or God's people just unprovoked. He did the same to Job. Job was just there maintaining his commitment to God when satan attacked. It is also a lesson to note that we do not have to be in sin or in rebellion for satan to attack. Satan is ruthless and merciless; his aim remains to steal, kill, and destroy. He did the same to Joseph when pharaoh's wife accused him falsely. Nevertheless, none of them compromised.

Back to king Jehoshaphat's story. This time when the Moabites and Ammonites with some of the Meunites advanced towards the Israelites, the king sought the Lord in prayer. In fact, he summoned all Israelites to gather by the Lord's temple. After the prayer, the Lord responded by assuring them that He would fight on their behalf. However, the Lord descended against their enemies after the Israelites lifted their voice in praise, thanksgiving, and worship. It would be best I highlighted these scriptures to really see the power of praise, thanksgiving, and worship in action. Here are the scriptures:

> *After this, the Moabites and Ammonites with some of the Meunites came to wage war against Jehoshaphat Some people came and told Jehoshaphat, "A vast army is coming against you from Edom, from the other side of the Dead Sea. It is already in Hazezon Tamar" (that is, En Gedi). Alarmed, Jehoshaphat resolved to inquire of the* LORD, *and he proclaimed a fast for all Judah. The people of Judah came together to seek help from the* LORD; *indeed, they came from every town in Judah to seek him.*

> *Then Jehoshaphat stood up in the assembly of Judah and Jerusalem at the temple of the* LORD *in the front of the new courtyard and said: "*LORD, *the God of our ancestors, are you not the God who is in heaven? You rule over all the kingdoms of the nations. Power and might are in your hand, and no one can withstand you. Our God, did you not drive out the inhabitants of this land before your people Israel and give it forever to the descendants of Abraham your friend? They have*

*lived in it and have built in it a sanctuary for your Name, saying, 'If calamity comes upon us, whether the sword of judgment, or plague or famine, we will stand in your presence before this temple that bears your Name and will cry out to you in our distress, and you will hear us and save us. 'But now here are men from Ammon, Moab and Mount Seir, whose territory you would not allow Israel to invade when they came from Egypt; so, they turned away from them and did not destroy them. See how they are repaying us by coming to drive us out of the possession you gave us as an inheritance. Our God, will you not judge them? For we have no power to face this vast army that is attacking us. We do not know what to do, but our eyes are on you. "All the men of Judah, with their wives and children and little ones, stood there before the LORD. Then the Spirit of the LORD came on Jahaziel son of Zechariah, the son of Benaiah, the son of Jeiel, the son of Mattaniah, a Levite and descendant of Asaph, as he stood in the assembly.*

*He said: "Listen, King Jehoshaphat and all who live in Judah and Jerusalem! This is what the LORD says to you: 'Do not be afraid or discouraged because of this vast army. For the battle is not yours, but God's. Tomorrow march down against them. They will be climbing up by the Pass of Ziz, and you will find them at the end of the gorge in the Desert of Jeruel. You will not have to fight this battle. Take up your positions; stand firm and see the deliverance the LORD will give you, Judah and Jerusalem. Do not be afraid; do not be discouraged. Go out to face them tomorrow, and the LORD will be with you.' Jehoshaphat bowed down with his face to the ground, and all the people of Judah and Jerusalem fell in worship before the LORD. Then some Levites from the*

*Kohathites and Korahites stood up and praised the LORD, the God of Israel, with a very loud voice.*

*Early in the morning they left for the Desert of Tekoa. As they set out, Jehoshaphat stood and said, "Listen to me, Judah and people of Jerusalem! Have faith in the LORD your God and you will be upheld; have faith in his prophets and you will be successful." After consulting the people, Jehoshaphat appointed men to sing to the LORD and to praise him for the splendor of his ¹holiness as they went out at the head of the army, saying: "Give thanks to the LORD, for his love endures forever." As they began to sing and praise, the LORD set ambushes against the men of Ammon and Moab and Mount Seir who were invading Judah, and they were defeated. The Ammonites and Moabites rose up against the men from Mount Seir to destroy and annihilate them. After they finished slaughtering the men from Seir, they helped to destroy one another.*

*When the men of Judah came to the place that overlooks the desert and looked toward the vast army, they saw only dead bodies lying on the ground; no one had escaped. So, Jehoshaphat and his men went to carry off their plunder, and they found among them a great amount of equipment and clothing and articles of value — more than they could take away. There was so much plunder that it took three days to collect it. On the fourth day they assembled in the Valley of Berakah, where they praised the LORD. This is why it is called the Valley of Berakah to this day.*

*Then, led by Jehoshaphat, all the men of Judah and Jerusalem returned joyfully to Jerusalem, for the LORD had given them cause to rejoice over their enemies. They entered Jerusalem and went to the temple of the LORD with harps and lyres and trumpets. The fear of God came on all the surrounding kingdoms when they heard how the LORD had fought against the enemies of Israel. And the kingdom of Jehoshaphat was at peace, for his God had given him rest on every side. (2 Chron. 20:1-30, NIV).*

The sincere change in Jehoshaphat's attitude towards God in 2 Chronicles 20, brought forth a war free victory. This is the same king who compromised with King Ahab and ignored God's instructions. Yet in this case, he sought the Lord, obeyed, but while still unsure of how God would fight his enemies, Jehoshaphat led the people to praise, thanksgiving and worship. The Lord broke through with tremendous victory! Hallelujah!

# SECTION III

# CONCLUSION

## RESPONSE TO REFLECTIVE QUESTIONS

# CHAPTER 16

# FAMILIARITY WITH GOD, WITH MAN, WITH YOUR ADVERSARY— ALL WILL SURPRISE YOU

≈

## Familiarity with God

It is my hope that you gathered some insights about familiarity. The main objectives for this book are to help you identify the subtle distraction of familiarity that can hinder your spiritual and natural growth and to help you attain fullness and maximization of your potential in God. The common factors to meet these two objectives are flexibility and adaptability.

When we are familiar with the things and the ways of God, we miss out on the "more" He would want to do in and for us. Although God never changes and He is the same yesterday, today and forever, the ways He goes about maturing us and training us differ depending on the lessons He wants us to learn and what He will do with us next. He is the God of more, when we are flexible and adaptable, often the outcome is exceedingly and abundantly above what we expected or know.

## Familiarity with fellow human beings

Familiarity with your fellow human, I would say from personal experience and life principle, is very crucial to submit and obey the leadership of the Holy Spirit on Whom you should be connected to and Whom you should serve. When you do not know your value, you can subject yourself to unnecessary conflict and harm from people. When people do not respect and appreciate the value you are to them, they can misuse, exploit, and betray you. People can also get so familiar with you that they lose respect for you and start taking you for granted, treating and talking to you any way they please. Most hurts and surprises are from those closest to you. This calls us to seek the Holy Spirit and ask Him to align you with the right people who bring the best out of you and help you fulfill your destiny. It also requires asking the Holy Spirit what activities you should be involved in. This can be challenging especially if you prone to helping people or if you are in ministry. More and more I am learning that being involved in multiple areas doing "good things" may not necessarily be God's will for you. Therefore, it is imperative that we utilize and appropriate every gift, talent, and resource with the help of the Holy Spirit and only support what God wants us to support. In addition, it is important to learn to set boundaries, say no, and decline offers that you know are outside God's will for you and are in themselves exploitative. If you submit to the Holy Spirit, the Holy Spirit will help you attain boldness and courage to speak out and say, "Enough!" He will also guide you to the right environment and bring you well-meaning people who will enrich your life and support your destiny.

## Satanic Patterns

Understanding satanic patterns and not giving them room to grow or manifest is very important in spiritual warfare. In a recent discussion with a mentee, I concluded that failure to recognize demonic patterns have been detrimental to most believers. As the mentee shared the experiences she had encountered within the week; the Holy Spirit quickly revealed that the mentee was encountering demonic patterns. This mentee had just recommitted to seeking God intentionally by reading the Bible, developing a structured prayer life, journaling her experiences with the Holy Spirit, learning how to hear God and applying what God had revealed to her. That same week she said out of nowhere she felt extremely tired. She did not feel like doing any of the above; in fact, most of days she got home and just went to bed. While at work, she got confronted by her coworkers, that same week, her adult son and daughter called her about to issues that she felt obligated to address in their home; crisis management!

If a believer is only left to the familiarity of satanic operations that are commonly known; they would not recognize that the above are really one demon of distraction manifesting in various forms. Notice the pattern from the mentee's experience. The same demon of distraction presented by first attacking her physically and emotionally, leading her to depression, depleted of both emotional and physical strength. Next, the same demon presented differently at work through; here the mentee concluded that the co-worker was just being mean. Oh no, it was the same demon of distraction. Then when her children called her in distress, that too was the same demonic spirit which created chaos in the family so that the mentee can utilize the time she had set part to seek God, to address the crisis and keep her from pursuing her God given assignment.

Glory be to God; by the end of that week, the mentee realized that she was in some form of spiritual warfare. I'm quoting her here; she said *"Pauline, once I realized what was going on I prayed and engaged in spiritual warfare prayer.* I prayed until I felt everything lift off! I feel much better today. I am ok". Fellowship with the Holy Spirit and prayer will aid us discern spiritual atmospheres, whether they godly or demonic. The mentee's experience also serves as a key example of being alert always as the Apostle Peter taught in 1 Peter 5:8; *Be sober, be vigilant; because your adversary the devil, as a roaring lion, walketh about, seeking whom he may devour. (KJV).* Prior to this Jesus warned believers to be wise; *behold, I send you out as sheep in the midst of wolves; so be shrewd as serpents and innocent as doves. Matthew 10:16 (NASB).*

The other lesson from the mentee's experience especially to those called into ministry of any type is "counting the cost and being living sacrifices each moment". You see when repeatedly attacked by demonic patterns, one can easily give up on pursuing their destiny in God or give in satan's antics. On counting the cost and being living sacrifices, the question poised is whether we have fully committed to the Call and whether we can press through to do what it takes no matter how much it costs us. The mentee had to push through the physical and emotional drain, get up and pray until breakthrough birthed forth. Her actions showed determination and rising above the distraction, pressing through her tired body to pray for herself, her coworkers and her children. Breakthrough came after travailing prayer. She prayed while still in her worst state yet came out victoriously. Can we be living sacrifices daily; stay alert, stay sober, press past our emotions, strengthen ourselves in the Lord and face demonic patterns head-on!

Then there are demonic cycles. When demonic influences seem to affect one generation to the next one or when they are cycles of negative occurrences, it is crucial to discern these as not mere coincidences. In 2001, I attended a wedding in Philadelphia Pennsylvania. As the wedding party lined up enter the reception hall, the maid of honor collapsed and was later pronounced dead. This was a young woman to have died. Later that evening as I joined the bereaved family for prayer, the sister commented that historically someone has died in their family each year on November 3rd. With that knowledge, I proceeded in prayer to break the curse of death in that family.

The key to dealing with demonic cycles is to identify the root of those patterns or door that allowed them to keep manifesting in someone's live. Most areas of deliverance are effective by first targeting root and not merely dealing with the symptoms followed by identifying and closing the entrance doors that were utilized by the demons. I believe this why Jesus asked the father of the young boy He delivered from epilepsy or seizures, "how long has he had this. The child's father responded, since birth, Mark 9:14-29. Jesus may have asked the question also because He had such compassion noticing that this child had been tormented for so long and it was time for his deliverance. I'm always touched and admonished by this; most of the accounts of Jesus, He always healed and delivered out of compassion, mercy and love. I strive daily to model Jesus. Jesus Christ is my model for ministry and for my life. Oops! Back to demonic cycles. If you see such cycles in your life or others, seek the help of your pastor or of qualified, reputable deliverance ministers to pray for you. If in need referral to deliverance ministries feel free email us through the contact menu at www.paulineadongo.com; we will provide you some references.

Satan on the other hand attacks in subtle ways too. I was just couching a mentee this afternoon that for a believer, satan may not use general temptations that you are familiar with. He knows you cannot steal or tell a lie, so he can attack you with anxiety and desire to serve in many ministries, through false beliefs that God did not hear your prayers or fears. Collectively, these are tactics used to distract you from pursuing God's assignment for you. If you are stuck on only the common, familiar tactics of satan, you will ignore other doors that he uses to attack. I encourage most believers and mentees to study all aspects of spiritual warfare to understand how satan's kingdom operates and how to affect its operation with the mighty authority of God's Kingdom, the power of the Name of Jesus, and the delivering power of the Blood of Jesus. There are great books and teachings on spiritual warfare; among my favorite is "Rules of Engagement" by Derek Prince.

## Conclusion

In conclusion, God is the ultimate estimate. To underestimate or quantify Him equals familiarity. I am learning in this journey that God is so balanced. Our God is beyond comparison. We must continually submit to God in total surrender to stay in the freshness of His glory. By doing this we are transformed from one glory to another; avoiding stagnation or staying the same. God does not move in familiarity. Although we are created in His image and He relates with us, God's ways are not our ways, neither are our thoughts His thoughts. In fact, our thoughts are foolish before Him. We cannot study God's ways let alone maneuver or manipulate Him; there are no seven steps to understanding God! The best solution to overcoming familiarity is submission and obedience.

> *Therefore, submit to God. Resist the devil, and he will flee from you. Draw nigh to God, and he will draw nigh to you. Cleanse your hands, you sinners; and purify your hearts, you double-minded. Lament and mourn and weep! Let your laughter be turned to mourning and your joy to gloom. Humble yourselves in the sight of the Lord, and He will lift you up (James 4:7–10, NJKV).*

CHAPTER 17

# REFLECTION

≈

"'For my thoughts are not your thoughts, neither are your ways my ways,' says the Lord. 'As the heavens are higher than the earth, so are my ways higher than your ways and my thoughts than your thoughts'" (Isa. 55: 8-9 NJKV).

The purpose of the reflections sections in each chapter was for personal reflection to help you identify areas that may be hindering fruitfulness or growth in your spiritual life. In this last chapter, take time to reflect and write down the areas and then let's just approach God in surrender:

If we confess our sins God is faithful and just to forgive our sins and cleanse us from all unrighteousness. I John 1:9, NKJV gives us the following prayer of repentance:

> *Father in the name of Jesus, I repent for (name the areas). I ask for your forgiveness. I renounce any rebellion or any stubbornness in me that hinders your move. I repent of any areas that I have assumed, ignored your instructions and just did what I wanted. Forgive me for moving by my emotions and in my strength and not seeking you out. Forgive me for taking you for granted and assume your ways. Forgiving for disobeying the Holy Spirit and*

*for restricting His move in my life. I command contrary spirit of rebellion out in Jesus Name.*

*I receive the Holy Spirit. Holy Spirit fill me a fresh; bring to remembrance the instructions I need to take and what I should do. Holy Spirit strengthen and help me pursue God's agenda for me by Your power. Lord I pray for restoration, fruitfulness and multiplication of the areas You will lead me to. I now surrender to You as my Potter as I remain a clay that is pliable and flexible in all you will do with me. In the name of Jesus Christ, I pray and believe. Amen.*

# CALL TO SALVATION & FILLING OF THE HOLY SPIRIT

≈

John 14:6-7: "Jesus said to him, 'I am the way, the truth, and the life. No one comes to the Father except through Me. If you had known Me, you would have known My Father also; and from now on you know Him and have seen Him'" (NKJV).

1 John 1:8-9: "If we say that we have no sin, we deceive ourselves, and the truth is not in us. If we confess our sins, God is faithful and just to forgive us our sins and to cleanse us from all unrighteousness" (NKJV).

Maybe you are at your wits end and you just want God to reach out to you and realign you to the marvelous plan He has for you. Invite Him to come in and take the lead by saying this prayer:

> Dear God, I come to you. I accept your Son Jesus Christ as my Lord and Savior. I believe that Jesus died and rose again for my sins that I may receive salvation. I therefore repent of my sins and ask for your forgiveness. I renounce sin. Lord Jesus now come to my life both in me and in everything that concerns me. Come in Lord Jesus and be Lord over my life and align me to the path and plan you have set for me. In the name of Jesus Christ, I pray. Amen.

Now invite the Holy Spirit who will serve as your helper and guide among many things in this new life. Say the following:

> Holy Spirit, I now welcome you to reside me and take over every aspect of my life. I submit to you Holy Spirit; guide me in knowledge, wisdom, revelation, and discernment and counsel to walk and accomplish the plan God has for me. Holy Ghost, fill me with your gifts that I may experience the fullness of God in this new life, in the name of Jesus I pray. Amen! Oh, beloved of the Lord, the Holy Spirit now resides in and with you. Watch out for what He is about to do!

With arms opened wide, welcome to the Kingdom of God! The next step is to look for a local church whose beliefs and doctrine align with the Word of God. I have already prayed that the Holy Spirit will connect you with the right believers who will help and guide you to maturity in Christ Jesus. On your end, set some time at least twice a day to pray and read the Bible. Prayer is simply talking to God. Ask the Holy Spirit to teach you how to pray, and then just pray. To start, pray when you first wake up and talk to God the way you talk to a friend you respected and be open to God, telling Him everything. If you can only pray 5 minutes twice a day, do that, then increase your prayer time daily. With time the Holy Spirit will mature your prayer life if you stay consistent.

You may read the Bible before or after your prayer time. Purchase a version or download a Bible app that you can easily understand such as the New Living Translation (NLT) or New International Version (NIV). I prefer the New King James Version (NKJV), but occasionally, I read other versions when I need clarification. When you are about to open the Bible, ask the Holy Spirit to illuminate and bring clarity to what you are about to read. The Holy Spirit is very good at this. This is His job—our helper. He reveals the truth to us. Start by reading the book of Proverbs and the Gospel of John. You can read one chapter of Proverbs when you wake up and a chapter from John before bedtime.

Purpose to memorize a scripture a day and meditate on the scripture that caught your attention. With time, the Word of God will become alive in your heart and in your thoughts. Before you know it, you would have read the entire Bible. When you get there start anew. By the help of the Holy Spirit this is how we grow; it takes personal responsibility.

# OTHER BOOKS BY THE AUTHOR

≈

**THE ALTERNATIVE PLAN** - Released in the summer of 2015, this book was written for young professionals in the work place as well as young adults from high school to those just launching into their first careers, to assure you that God can still realign your life to fit the plan He intended for you. This book was written to those questioning their future, and it ministers to the wounded and those seeking security in their lives. This book highlights the lies Satan uses to sabotage the plan of God for you. It demonstrates God's ability to clean up and restore to fullness, even the greatest mess. Through reading this book, may you receive salvation, healing, deliverance, restoration, and restitution in the Name of Jesus through His Blood! The purpose of this book is to bring hope to the reader and provide direction on how to get back to the plan God intended for you.

ISBN-978-0-9898247-6-7. Hardcover. 55 pages

# CALLED TO MINISTRY,
# NOW WHAT!

☐ ☐ ☐ ☐ ☐

*A foundational guide to your journey in ministry*

PAULINE
ADONGO

Each of us was born with gifts and talents. Some still struggle with identifying their gifts, others struggle with how to develop those gifts. In this book, you will detect possible clues that are linked to your gifts and how they manifest. Throughout the book, you, will be shown how to identify and develop your gifts and talents; in partnership with the Holy Spirit and with man (God appointed mentors). This book is for EVERY believer because all believers are ministers. This book is for those contemplating pursuing ministries but who have no clue what to do; for Ministers in Training or ministry interns, for ANY church worker; for deacons, elders, ministers and pastors. It is a foundational manual: 101 in ministry, but the Spirit inspired words in this book can be applied IN ALL vocational areas including church and the workforce. Be equipped, the harvest is plenteous!

ISBN-978-1-5127-2760-9. Hardcover. 104 pages

MINISTRY beyond THE PULPIT

You are a Minister wherever you are

PAULINE ADONGO

Titles and talents are NOT prerequisites for service. Each believer is uniquely and individually gifted by God and has the capacity and capability to minister to others. Jesus Christ in His mandate to the His followers said "go ye"; there are no special titles or designations tied to this mandate other that "those who believe" (Mark 16:14-20). The main objective of this book is to encourage each believer to recognize the platform God has given them to accomplish the Great Commission. This platform may be a career, vocation, business, home environment or department in a church. This platform is what I refer to as "your pulpit". Each believer has one. Once you have recognized your pulpit, I discuss how both natural gifts, talents and spiritual gifts can be applied collectively to minister to others. The harvest is still plenteous. Having been already empowered by Jesus, let us join in gathering the harvest. Go ahead and minister wherever you are!

ISBN-978-1-3127-4316-6. Hardcover.55 pages

# PRAYER IS SIMPLY
## TALKING TO GOD
It's not complicated. Just talk to God

PAULINE ADONGO

Prayer itself, as well as the approach to prayer and attitude towards prayer are simplified in this book, granting readers the freedom to pray. Prayer, when rendered to the Holy Spirit, produces more. Among the key topics that are discussed in this book are: Aspects of prayers, Common misconceptions about prayer, Benefits of prayer, Holy Spirit led prayer -the role of the Holy Spirit in prayer, praying from a victorious position in spiritual warfare, how to pray while waiting for the answer, how to incorporate prayer in daily routine. These have been shared to free the reader to simply talk to God.

ISBN-978-1-5127-6698-1. Hardcover.94 pages

Books can be purchased from
www.paulineadongo.com

# ABOUT THE AUTHOR

≈

Pauline Adongo believes in prayer and power of the Holy Spirit to bring salvation, healing, deliverance, restoration, and restitution to the Body of Christ and to the nations. Her greatest desire is to see all mankind edified in God by encouraging and equipping the Body of Christ to know their identity and the authority that they have as children of God. Pauline's passion for God stems from her understanding of God's love of salvation and deliverance. She is a testimony of God's grace and mercy; seeing God's perfect plan redirect her life. Pauline currently works and lives in Pennsylvania, USA. To God be the Glory, great things He is doing!

**CONTACT INFORMATION or TO INVITE PAULINE FOR SPEAKING ENGAGEMENTS**
PAULINE ADONGO
THE MINISTRY OF JESUS CHRIST INTERNATIONAL INC.
P.O BOX 2572, WEST CHESTER, PA 19380
EMAIL: padongomjc@gmail.com
WEBSITE: www.paulineadongo.com
Facebook, Instagram, YouTube and Twitter

Printed in the United States
By Bookmasters